CONTENTS

Welcome	2
What you need to do to hold a GraveTalk event	3
Take away sheet for participants to keep	11
Theological reflections on death and dying	12
Practical information	15
Understanding grief	23
Useful websites	27
Books	31

Facilitator's Guide

WELCOME

There are signs throughout our culture that people are beginning to talk about death, dying and funerals. The Church of England conducts around 3,300 funerals each week and for generations the church has been helping people prepare for dying, remember loved ones at funeral services, and has supported them on their journey of grief and remembering. We have lots of experience to draw on.

GraveTalk is a simple way to help people in your community get together and talk about death, dying and funerals in the relaxed easy context of a café space. It has been tried and tested over the past two years and proved successful and popular.

This guide is to help you set up and run your own GraveTalk event. It has practical tips and ideas about the event as well as some background theological thinking. However, we encourage you to adapt GraveTalk to your own context.

This guide also contains practical information about the arrangements that need to be made when someone dies and a short article about grief which you are free to reproduce. There is also a list of useful websites and books.

GraveTalk is one of the resources that has been developed as part of the Church of England's work around funerals and dying.

For more information visit www.gravetalk.org

FUNERALS

WHAT YOU NEED TO DO TO HOLD A GRAVETALK EVENT

1. Think

Your first task is to think through the significance of death and dying for yourself and your church community.

- We recommend you spend some time thinking about death and dying. You might find it useful to do a reflective exercise, or meditate on the death of Jesus, or remember before God those who have died. The important thing is that you can be at ease with personal issues around death and dying, so that you are able to respond appropriately to whatever comes up in the group.

- Observe your church community and think about its relationship to death and dying. When do people talk about death? Who is involved when somebody dies?

- Consider planning a sermon series, magazine article or a study session for a small group around death, dying and funerals.

- Take time to look at the GraveTalk cards and become familiar with them.

> *'I think a general discussion group would be a good idea. You don't have to do it with the whole congregation – just a dozen at a time. I think that would be a good idea.'*
>
> *Research respondent*

FACILITATOR'S GUIDE

2. Organise

- Decide the date and time for your event.
  - GraveTalk can be a day-time or evening event, during the week or at a weekend. Allow between 1½ and 2 hours.
- Decide who you are going to invite. It might be best to run the first event for your congregation, before organising a wider event in the community.
- Decide the venue for your event – think about the atmosphere and space.
  - GraveTalk can be in a church hall, or in a local café, pub or other community space. Remember it is a space for refreshments and talk, so should be relaxed and comfortable.
  - The venue should allow for people to sit around small tables, in groups of three or four, with hospitality such as tea/coffee and cake.
- Decide on the leadership – you need at least one facilitator and a host, neither of whom need to be ordained.
  - The facilitator[s] need to be comfortable talking about death, able to listen well and steer conversation. They don't need to give answers.
  - The host[s] need to be good at hospitality.
- Ensure that the church leadership is informed.

> FUNERALS

- Plan the promotion of your event. In addition to your regular publicity, there are special GraveTalk posters and postcards which you can order to your requirements at www.churchprinthub.org
- Think through how to communicate clearly that this event is for those wishing to discuss death, dying and funerals. Consider what provision is available for those with personal issues around bereavement and/or with a terminal diagnosis.
- Make sure you have enough GraveTalk cards for each table to have a good selection of questions. Make sure there is at least one from each section. Think about how to distribute them.
- Pray and ask others to pray for GraveTalk.

3. Run your event

- Pay careful attention to the practical details. Good hospitality can contribute towards a safe atmosphere in which participants can feel comfortable talking about death and dying.
- Look through the materials beforehand. Decide whether you are going to use the materials and programme we suggest; and if you are going to make changes, decide which ones.
- Don't forget to give everybody a reflection sheet to take away at the end, and invite them to leave their contact details for follow-up on the way out, if they wish to do so.
- You might also like to make sure there is a range of information from local organisations available.

Facilitator's Guide

4. Organise repeat events

Consider whether you want a second event, remembering that:

- it's not a course – it's a conversation.
- it could be for a different group of people.
- it could be at a different time.
- it could be a regular event in church/community life.
- it could be in partnership with your local Funeral Director/residential home/chaplaincy/ecumenical colleagues.

> 'Very, very easy. Just set the plans, first one we had was in Caffè Nero …The local press publicised it … I think about seventeen or eighteen people for the first one …
> a really interesting broad range of ages, you know, right across the spectrum …
> we then followed that up with one in the library, which again we had some people who'd come to the first one then came to the second one.'
>
> *Vicar, Cumbria*

FUNERALS

General guidance on how to run your event

You will need to decide for yourself the best way to run an event in your specific context. But if you would like a structure to work to, then we suggest something similar to this:

1830 Facilitators/hosts set up space and display [if used].

1900 Arrive, mingle, coffee.

1930 Convene. Welcome and short prayer. Explanation from facilitator about GraveTalk and the shape of the evening.

1945 Break into groups of three to six, each sitting around a table. Turn over one of the cards provided and use it to trigger a conversation. If people get stuck, move onto a second card. Make sure all have opportunity to talk, and ensure that conversation doesn't get 'stuck' on one individual or one topic. *There is no need to go through all the cards.*

2045 Gather for a period of shared reflection using the sheet (see next section), then a closing prayer or short act of worship.

Include a sheet at the back of event for people to put their personal details if they'd like follow-up information.

You might have a display of other materials/books available.

Make sure people know about www.churchofenglandfunerals.org and the pages about planning funerals.

FACILITATOR'S GUIDE

Prayer space

You might like to set up a display similar to that in the photograph on page 10 of this pack. Nearby you could place some candles or stones which people can place as prayer symbols.

For a more formal **opening prayer**, we suggest something like this:

> As your local parish church, we have organised this session of GraveTalk so that people of all faiths and doubts can take part in an open conversation about death, dying and funerals. This is my prayer for our time together, to which you are welcome, if you wish, to add your amen.
>
> *'Almighty God, you raised your Son, Jesus Christ, from the dead. In his earthly life, he wept at the death of his friend, Lazarus. Open our hearts this morning/afternoon/evening that we might listen to one another in compassion and hope, as we explore our lives in the context of death. In his name, we pray. Amen.'*

We suggest that you also give some advice about the nature of the conversation, along these lines:

> We are meeting for an open conversation about death, dying and funerals. People may wish to share personal thoughts and feelings, ask questions and draw on their experience of life. Please respect the trust that we place in one another for the duration of this time, and afterwards, if you do refer back to the contribution that anyone else made, do so in a generalised manner that does not identify the person.

Using the GraveTalk cards

Remind people again that the cards are conversation starters, not questions with right answers. Respect people's answers and thoughts and allow conversation to flow naturally. If you only look at one card, that's fine!

> 'I gave it to them [the PCC] and I went and made coffee while they started discussing it. And I just couldn't shut them up. They thought it was great. When I came to draw them to a conclusion, they wanted to carry on. They thought it was absolutely brilliant. I was really surprised.'
>
> *Vicar, Cumbria*

Closing the session

At the close of the session, we suggest you thank people for their participation, and draw their attention to the follow-up sheet. You might wish to provide a very brief concluding act of worship. This may include a period of silence, during which people may reflect on their personal thoughts, both private and spoken. You may wish to lead with a prayer similar to the one on page 10. Finally, we suggest that, as people come to leave, they have the opportunity to come forward to a central spot for an activity such as lighting a candle or leaving a prayer request.

As we conclude our time together, let us be silent for a couple of minutes, following which I will lead in a prayer, to which, if you wish, you are welcome to add your amen.

'Heavenly Father, creator of all life, we bless you for the mystery of life and death, and for the promise of everlasting life through our Saviour, Jesus Christ. Amongst those who have died, we thank you in particular for all those whom we have loved, and who have loved us. Reflecting on their lives, grant us courage and wisdom to follow the way of Jesus Christ, who came that we might have life, and have it abundantly. In his name we pray. Amen.'

NB: the base fabric is black, and the overlay is yellow to symbolise the tension between thanksgiving and loss. Colour photo available on www.churchsupporthub/GraveTalk

TAKE AWAY SHEET FOR YOU TO KEEP

The GraveTalk session aims to encourage us to consider death, an aspect of our lives we may not always like to think about. Having the opportunity to talk about death, dying and funerals should help us to carry on thinking about it and the following questions may help you to shape what will be one of the most significant events of our lives for ourselves and others. You may like to make some notes after each question to assist you.

1. What was, for you, the most significant part of the conversations during our GraveTalk session?

2. Are there any matters you would like to explore further? Or is there something in particular you would like to find out more about?

3. Are there any practical things you need to do?

4. If now or later, you need to discuss anything further, can you identify the most appropriate person for you to talk to?

Downloadable from www.churchprinthub.com/funerals

THEOLOGICAL REFLECTIONS ON DEATH AND DYING

By The Revd David Primrose, Director of Transforming Communities, Diocese of Lichfield

GraveTalk is a ministry of the Church of England for those of all faiths and doubts. These sessions are an opportunity for people to articulate their own thoughts and feelings, ask their own questions and share their own experience in a relaxed environment. As a local parish church, you host these events and allow people to talk about their own understandings of issues around death, dying and funerals. Hence it is within the existing preaching and teaching ministry of the church, rather than at GraveTalk, that people have the opportunity to learn traditional Christian teaching on these matters. For example, death, dying and funerals may be an occasional topic of sermons during the months before and after running GraveTalk. The following paragraphs highlight matters that participants may talk about during GraveTalk sessions and which you may wish to address elsewhere. Some scriptural references are included.

Death and dying are such a fundamental aspect of life that they have a direct impact on many contemporary issues debated within the church. Between churches and within churches, there are a variety of positions adopted on ethical matters such as assisted dying, organ donation, cloning, abortion, suicide, capital punishment and pacifism. In engaging with these issues, Brendan McCarthy, who advises the Archbishops' Council, suggests that we apply Christian moral teaching

FUNERALS

to the principles of affirming life, caring for the vulnerable, building a caring society and respecting the individual.

Central to the Gospels is the proclamation that God raised Jesus from death (Matthew 28; Mark 16; Luke 24; John 20). The early church taught that his resurrection is a model for our resurrection (1 Corinthians 15; 1 Thessalonians 4:13ff). We look forward to his second coming, when God will transform the whole of his creation in accordance with his will (Revelation 21). Within this framework, we believe each person has a single life-span on this earth, which, through God's grace, is the basis for the life to come (Luke 16:19ff). Most people find it easiest to understand death as the point of transition from this life, bounded in time, to eternal life, which lies outside of time.

Sometimes people have an interest in using spiritualist means to try to contact those who have died. This has always been outside the teaching of the church, being rejected on theological or psychological grounds.

The church holds that the essence of God is love (1 John 4:7ff) and that he will judge between right and wrong (Matthew 25:31ff). While the church agrees that salvation is through Jesus Christ (John 14:1ff), this is interpreted in different ways. For some a personal faith in Jesus Christ is a prerequisite for salvation, whilst others hold that all will be saved. All believe in heaven, and for some this goes along with a belief in hell, to which others would add purgatory.

In the face of death, many people take a fatalistic approach, asserting the role of luck. Christian teaching embraces the sovereignty of God along with personal responsibility (Matthew 25:1ff). There is an obligation to use wisely the opportunities that we do have without exaggerating human autonomy (Luke 12:13ff).

Jesus is the resurrection and the life (John 11:25ff), and nothing can separate us from the love of God (Romans 8:38ff).

Helping people express their thoughts

Often people don't have the language to say deep things. They may say things that the facilitators or others find strange. It is important not to laugh at or dismiss or correct the things people say, however strange you may think they are. It's better to say, 'That's interesting – tell me more about what you're thinking.' That often leads to some much deeper insights and opens up conversation. That's the aim of GraveTalk.

> 'We did one in our community café, and there were ten or eleven, it was really nice. The conversation flowed, and they liked the questions and there were a lot of comments that it was very helpful.'
>
> *Vicar, Hampshire*

FUNERALS

PRACTICAL INFORMATION
What to do when someone dies
Overview

There are three things you must do in the first few days after someone dies.

1. Get a medical certificate — you'll get this from a doctor (GP or at a hospital) and you need one to register the death.
2. Register the death within five days of the death — you'll then get the documents you need for the funeral.
3. Arrange the funeral — you can use a funeral director or do it yourself.

You can deal with their will, money and property later.

Registering the death

If the death has been reported to a coroner you can't register the death until the coroner gives permission.

Who can register the death, the documents you'll need and documents you'll get depend on the circumstances of the death. Use the 'Register a Death' tool on the UK Government website (www.gov.uk/register-a-death) to find out what you need to do.

Facilitator's Guide

When a death is reported to a coroner

A doctor may report the death to a coroner if:

- the cause of death is unknown.
- the death was violent or unnatural.
- the death was sudden and unexplained.
- the person who died was not visited by a medical practitioner during their final illness.
- the medical certificate isn't available.
- the person who died wasn't seen by the doctor who signed the medical certificate within fourteen days before death or after they died.
- the death occurred during an operation or before the person came out of anaesthetic.
- the medical certificate suggests the death may have been caused by an industrial disease or industrial poisoning.

The coroner may decide that the cause of death is clear. In this case:

1. The doctor signs a medical certificate.
2. You take the medical certificate to the registrar.
3. The coroner issues a certificate to the registrar stating a post-mortem isn't needed.

FUNERALS

Post-mortems

The coroner may decide a post-mortem is needed to find out how the person died. This can be done either in a hospital or mortuary.

You can't object to a coroner's post-mortem, but if you've asked, the coroner must tell you (and the person's GP) when and where the examination will take place.

After the post-mortem

The coroner will release the body for a funeral once they have completed the post-mortem examinations and no further examinations are needed.

If the body is released with no inquest, the coroner will send a form (Pink Form B / form 100) to the registrar stating the cause of death.

The coroner will also send a Certificate of Coroner (Cremation form 6) if the body is to be cremated.

If the coroner decides to hold an inquest

A coroner must hold an inquest if the cause of death is still unknown, or if the person:

- possibly died a violent or unnatural death.
- died in prison or police custody.

You can't register the death until after the inquest. The coroner is responsible for sending the relevant paperwork to the registrar.

Although the death can't be registered until after the inquest, the coroner can give you a certificate to prove the person is dead. When the inquest is over the coroner will tell the registrar what to put in the register.

Arranging the funeral

The funeral can usually only take place after the death has been registered. Most people use a funeral director, although you can arrange a funeral yourself. You can also contact a vicar or other local minister.

Funeral directors

Get more than one quote to compare costs. You should choose a funeral director who's a member of either:

- the National Association of Funeral Directors, or
- the Society of Allied and Independent Funeral Directors.

Both organisations have codes of practice and have to give you a price list when asked.

Some local councils run their own funeral services, e.g. non-religious burials. The British Humanist Association can also help with non-religious funerals.

FUNERALS

Arranging the funeral yourself

Contact the cemeteries and crematoriums department of your local council to arrange a funeral yourself.

Funeral costs

Funeral costs can include:

- funeral director fees.
- things the funeral director pays for on your behalf (called 'disbursements' or 'third party costs'), e.g. crematorium or cemetery fees, a newspaper announcement about the death.
- local authority burial or cremation fees.

Funeral directors may list all these costs in their quote.

Paying for a funeral

The funeral can be paid for:

- by you or other family members or friends.
- from a financial scheme the person had taken out such as a funeral plan or insurance policy.
- from money from the person's estate (e.g. savings) – getting access to this is called applying for a 'grant of representation' (sometimes called 'applying for probate').

You can apply for a Funeral Payment (see www.gov.uk/funeral-payments/overview) if you have difficulty paying for the funeral.

Facilitator's Guide

Moving a body out of England or Wales

You need to get permission from a coroner to move a body for a funeral abroad. Apply at least four days before you want the body to be moved.

Find a local coroner using the 'Find a coroner' search on The Coroners' Society website: www.coronersociety.org.uk

Organisations you need to contact

Most local councils run a service called *Tell Us Once* — it reports a death to most government organisations in one go.

The registrar will explain your options for using *Tell Us Once* and give you a unique reference number to use the service.

Tell Us Once will notify:

- HM Revenue & Customs (HMRC) — to deal with tax and cancel benefits.

- Department of Work and Pensions (DWP) — to cancel benefits, e.g. income support.

- Driver and Vehicle Licensing Agency (DVLA) — to cancel a driving licence.

- Passport Office — to cancel a passport.

- The local council — to cancel housing benefit, council tax benefit, a Blue Badge, inform council housing services and remove the person from the electoral register.

FUNERALS

Banks and other financial organisations

Contact the person's bank or mortgage, pension or insurance providers to close or change the details of their accounts.

Dealing with tax and benefits

If you have used the *Tell Us Once* service the following organisations should contact you to deal with tax and benefits.

HM Revenue & Customs (HMRC)

HMRC will normally send you form R27 if the person paid tax on their income. This is used to work out:

- what tax HMRC need to collect or repay.
- whether you need to fill in a Self Assessment tax return on the person's behalf, e.g. when the estate continues to receive income.

You can also use HMRC's bereavement tool to work out which forms to fill in and where to send them.

Inheritance Tax may be due on the person's estate after they die.

HMRC Pay As You Earn and Self Assessment
Telephone: 0300 200 3300
Monday to Friday, 8am to 8pm
Saturday, 8am to 4pm

Contact HMRC if they haven't been in touch within thirty days of registering the death.

Facilitator's Guide

National Insurance (NI) contributions office

Contact the NI contributions office to cancel the person's NI payments if they were self-employed or paying voluntary NI.

Child Benefit Office

Contact the Child Benefit Office if a child or the parent dies. Do this within eight weeks of the death.

Tax Credit Office

Contact the Tax Credit Office if your partner or a child you're responsible for dies. Do this within one month of the death.

Department of Work and Pensions (DWP)

Contact the bereavement service to cancel the person's benefits. They'll also check if you're eligible for help with funeral costs or other benefits.

DWP Bereavement Service
Telephone: 0845 606 0265
Textphone: 0845 606 0285

FUNERALS

UNDERSTANDING GRIEF
By Manjula Patel from the Murray Hall Trust

What is grief?

Grief is a normal reaction to loss and bereavement: it is inevitable to mourn the loss of someone you love and care about. Grief is very personal and highly individual — for everyone it will be a unique experience. There is no right or wrong way to go through grief and for everyone it will be different. It might be helpful to know there are different aspects of grief that people may go through that are normal. These include:

- denial and disbelief that the loss/death has occurred.
- anger about what has happened and asking, 'why?'
- bargaining – wanting to change what has happened.
- sadness – overwhelming sorrow about what has happened.
- acceptance – finding a way to accept what has happened.

Individuals may experience some or all of these feelings and there is no order to how people will go through grief, they may overlap with each other and there is no time limit to how long each aspect will last. Grief is a painful process and its intensity may be dependent on the significance of the relationship with the deceased individual. Grieving is a rollercoaster of emotions that will involve sadness, fear, anger, despair, helplessness and disorientation.

Living with grief

Everyone experiencing grief need the support of other people, someone to talk with and share the burden of your loss. Even when you do not feel like being in company it is important to have the support of others around you as part of your healing process. Sometime you may want to share your experience of grief with others who have been bereaved within your own social networks or your local church, or you may want to access local bereavement support groups, telephone support or online forums.

Grieving involves more than coming to terms with the loss of 'the other' – it is also the 'loss of self', especially when your identity has been entwined with the person who has died. Death also makes us face our own mortality, and losses make us question the meaning of our own lives.

A personal faith may be a source of comfort and drawing on spiritual activities such as praying, meditating and attending church may offer solace. It is not unusual during times of loss to find yourself questioning your faith and you may find it helpful to talk to a vicar or a member of your faith community.

There are physical symptoms to grief, including loss of appetite and lack of sleep, fatigue and tiredness. It is important to look after yourself by eating regular meals, exercising and getting enough sleep. Though the sadness of losing someone you love never goes away

FUNERALS

completely, sometimes people can become stuck in their grief and you may need to seek help from others such as your GP or bereavement counsellor.

The death of a loved one is life-changing. For some people it has significantly shaped their future and given them a deeper appreciation for life, with a new understanding of being able to empathise with others in their pain and suffering.

Will I forget them?

A fear that many people have is that they will forget their loved one in time. This is a normal emotion and a part of adjusting your life after a bereavement.

There is growing recognition that people who are bereaved continue to integrate into their life narrative the significant relationships of their lives, be they dead or alive. In this sense there is a continued relationship, and it is natural that you will find yourself talking about them in everyday conversations and remembering them on significant dates, as well as reminders through countless images you may have of them in photographs, videos and in significant places and objects of meaning.

Grief, remembering and church

Finding a space to sit and be with thoughts and memories can be really important, whether a death has occurred recently or long ago. It doesn't matter if the funeral happened locally or far away, in a crematorium or at a graveside or in a woodland – a local church can provide a really special place of quiet. Some churches are able to offer a place to light candles or to leave prayers, and this is very helpful for many people.

There are also particular times when memories can be painful – Christmas, Mothering Sunday and Valentine's Day are all times when the celebrations all around can throw loss into sharp focus. Many churches find offering special services around these times can be helpful.

After a funeral, the friendship and support offered by a local church may well encourage people to come to worship services, especially if they are invited and even accompanied by someone. Congregations play a really important part in reaching out in welcome, and helping people to discover the great love of God revealed in Jesus Christ, which gives them hope and comfort.

USEFUL WEBSITES

Sources of support and information on specific issues.

Age UK
Age UK has useful information about making a will and a Lifebook, where you record the practical details of your life and where you keep certain documents. You can order a printed copy of the book on **0845 685 1061** and quote reference **ALL 721**, or email for an electronic copy.
www.ageuk.org.uk/home-and-care/home-safety-and-security/lifebook

Bereavement UK
Bereavement UK is a national organisation that offers information about death, dying, bereavement, funerals and self-help counselling.
www.bereavementuk.co.uk

Bereavement Advice Centre
The Bereavement Advice Centre supports and advises people on what they need to do after a death.
www.bereavementadvice.org

Centre for Death and Society
The Centre for Death and Society is hosted at Bath University and is UK's only centre devoted to the study and research of social aspects of death, dying and bereavement.
www.bath.ac.uk/cdas

Christian Legacy
The website offers information about leaving legacies and writing wills.
www.christianlegacy.org.uk

Church of England
The Church of England funerals website offers information about funerals and planning a funeral service.
www.churchofenglandfunerals.org

Compassionate Communities
Compassionate Communities has stories, short films and other information relating to end of life care issues.
www.compassionatecommunities.org.uk

Conversations for Life
Conversations for Life encourages conversation about death and dying.
www.conversationsforlife.co.uk

CRUSE Bereavement Care
Cruse provides information and support services for bereaved people.
www.crusebereavementcare.org.uk

Death Café
Death Café encourages people around the world to plan events to encourage discussions about death. The website offers practical advice and resources for planning a death café.
www.deathcafe.com

FUNERALS

Dying Matters
The Dying Matters Coalition is hosted by the National Council of Palliative Care. The Dying Matters website has a wide range of resources to help people start conversations about dying, death and bereavement, which include leaflets, posters, postcards, event planning packs and short films.
www.dyingmatters.org

End of Life Care for All
The National End of Life Care Programme has developed a public access e-learning resource, designed to enhance the training and education of all those involved in delivering end of life care.
www.e-lfh.org.uk/projects/end-of-life-care-(public-access)

Good Funeral Guide
The Good Funeral Guide is independent of the funeral industry and is dedicated to supporting, empowering and representing the interests of dying and bereaved people living in the UK. The website offers practical advice when planning a funeral.
www.goodfuneralguide.co.uk

Macmillan Cancer Support
Macmillan Cancer Support has a variety of information relating to cancer, including end of life issues and bereavement.
www.macmillan.org.uk

Macmillan Learn Zone
Macmillan Cancer Support provides a learning zone to find out more about helping yourself or others.
www.learnzone.org.uk

Marie Curie Cancer Care
Marie Curie Cancer Care has a variety of resources that include leaflets, booklets and short film guides about looking after someone at home when they are dying.
www.mariecurie.org.uk

Open to Hope
An online forum to support people living with loss and give them an opportunity to share their stories.
www.opentohope.com

UK Government
Practical information about what to do when someone dies, from registering a death to bereavement benefits advice.
www.gov.uk/browse/births-deaths-marriages/death

Winston's Wish
Winston's Wish offers practical support and guidance for bereaved children, their families and professionals.
www.winstonswish.org.uk

FUNERALS

BOOKS

Mike Riddell (2010) Sacred Journey: Spiritual Wisdom for Times of Transition (SPCK)

Sue Brayne (2010) The D-Word: Talking about Dying (Continuum)

Jeremy Brooks (2013) Heaven's Morning Breaks (Kevin Mayhew)

Ruth Burgess (2013) Saying Goodbye: Resources for Funerals, Scattering Ashes and Remembering (Wild Goose)

Marie De Hennezel (1998) Intimate Death: How the Dying Teach Us to Live (Sphere)

James Woodward (2005) Befriending Death (SPCK)

City of Gold: Impressions of Heaven (1997) CD and book featuring the words of Adrian Plass, John Bunyan, C.S. Lewis, J. John and others (Gold Records)

Church House Publishing
Church House
Great Smith Street
London SW1P 3AZ

ISBN 978 0 7151 4702 3

Published 2015 by Church House Publishing

Copyright © The Archbishops' Council 2015

All rights reserved. Pages 11, 23, 24, 25 & 26 only may be copied freely for local non-commercial use. Otherwise, no part of this publication may be reproduced or stored or transmitted by any means or in any form, electronic or mechanical, including photocopying, recording, or any information storage and retrieval system without written permission, which should be sought from copyright@churchofengland.org

Printed in the UK